NO
VACANCIES
IN
HELL

NO VACANCIES IN HELL

Poems by
Daniel Mark Epstein

LIVERIGHT

New York

Acknowledgement is gratefully made to the following magazines in which these poems first appeared: The New Yorker, *which published "Miss Ellie's 78th Spring Party";* The Virginia Quarterly Review, *which published "The Exile's Letter";* The Nation, *which published "The Secret" and "Lady in Her Bath";* Poet Lore, *which published "Letter Concerning the Yellow Fever";* Michigan Quarterly, *which published "Requiem for Christine Latrobe";* and The Northwest Review, *which published "The Search."*

1. 9 8 7 6 5 4 3 2 1

Library of Congress Catalog Card Number: 73-82426

ISBN: 0–87140–574–1

Designed by Betty Binns
MANUFACTURED IN THE UNITED STATES OF AMERICA

Contents

for Carolyn Monka

SEVEN

WOMEN

Al Que Quiere

Honor I have none but love plenty.

Sometimes like a monk shot out of his cave,
inner eye dead set on a starred chalice,
silver thistle points,
bright streaks pulse in the distance
above all distance. Or more like

some grizzled trapper come
down out of the barren crags for supplies,
wrapped in fox-skin, bob-cat and ermine,
shocked by the cold and the hard lights of town.
Beating at the doors of old friends

that open a crack and slam. Each year
I have less to give them.
I stop young women in the streets
and ask my most precious questions.
And they ask in return, nothing,
and even this is too much.

Scorpio

I loved a girl who was in love with death
and made him a song she would not sing to me.
My child lay wound in a golden maze of bunting
in her arms, my gift to her, and a still unopened rose.
These could not match death's promises.

"This year is as hard as life by our calendar,
with a black winter at either end of it.
Oh you that so flatter the mystery
but love your answers more,
if the earth should spin at random in the night
and this high room we lie in turn on its stem,
will you know dawn from evening when we rise?"

   "It must be the strength of his arms,"
I said, "and eyes that never turn aside."

"No. It is his silent listening," she replied.

I loved a girl who was in love with death
and made him a song she would not sing to me
or speak, or hum, despite
the knot of promise in the boy child's limbs,
the spiral introversion of the rose.

The Secret

She would not pick up stones
even the most beautiful ones
or keep them, let alone
keep them, they never look
the same on the windowsill, or in
a bowl as in the brook,
she would not
pick flowers either
and they grow
so much faster than stones.

Corona

Telling you my love is like trying
to describe the sun in detail,
and it blots hell out of the picture.
Threshed gold. Threshold of your hair,
sun-bedazzled, be-damned, like trying

like a child Sherlock holding the lens above a leaf
at noon, diamond-like convergence on this dot
that saffrons a halo at the edges, then
browns, and a splash of ink-blot shaped space
where the shot blade frazzles and turns back.

Yet if the sun goes out of its way, braiding the best
rays into my lady's hair and makes her shine, who
am I to deny or make light of this, old lover
or new? Clouds hang rain-prone and the sun
opens itself to us only a handful of times:

hold them hard love, and you might not hear
behind you, the nimbus detonating rapid-fire.

Celeste

No fair end to the madder blue of your eyes,
blue currents of your veins race through my sheets
and these wholly unaccountable passions:
a brace of tigers pawing at the stars.

Though we may find no moment right
for death where we go walking,
murder, Celeste, is on my mind,
your life not worth its image on my blade.

The Last Look

When you left in October, I slept
three nights in my clothes to keep the chill away.
Then so many lives passed I can't count them,
ambiguous dawns and sunsets,
the figure's outline on the moonlit beach
in shadowy motion looked the same
wading in, or out of the sea. And you lived
lives apart from me, I remembered all but that
you are a woman. In August you returned, unfaithful,
my dream of you, a blue-white star
frozen in a ripple of ice, shattered.
A fist rammed through the window pane,
blood stained the silver spiderweb of cracks,
slivers, as in the old wives' tale
rushed upstream to the heart. Forgive me,
I was a child again, left a dead man's problem,
tears the only sign of life on a barren face.
When all I could feel for you was a cool rain
lightening the ponderous thunder in my heart.

The Search

In my new house, windows at eyelevel
with the sun at dusk stare hard at me,
lone gull in a glass maze
beating limp wings against the solid glare.
Landlocked. I haven't been able to feel at home
and your letter ripped open on my desk
asking me to look for you, set me crazy.

For a day you were here five days ago,
the spray of purple ironweed
browns in an earthen jug with two other wildflowers
you picked, whose names I have forgotten.
I have forgotten your names, those
given you by love, and I'm lost,
lone fool in a glass cage,
disjointed puppet hanging in a jar deadpan,
our loves of the past fall so far behind me
that the brightest leaf now descending
will not touch warm ground.

A night of sitting alone, falling
asleep, falling into tears
until the moon through the broken window grew
transparent, lost its edge
and the craters flooded with skylight.
You were the only shadow thrown on my body
at daybreak, when the mist uncovered
fields splashed red with poppies, flying. Catch
hold!

I cannot speak in miracles, Pamela,
pin-point, counterpoint
the shifting center of flawless crystal
where we stood. You must look for yourself.

Lady In Her Bath

All day has been morning. Birds rattle,
the trees stock still beneath them,
leaves blue in the white air. The girl bathes
gracefully, her own epiphany,
all of cool circles in water.
Does a god move in her limbs or is there
a god in the air around her guiding them? Or
is all light self-radiant?

She draws her body slowly through the pool
bathing him from her, his flesh
and vision. It is this freedom
that is divine in her momentarily,
flash of her smooth limbs, white, whole.

The eyes are violet. Her eyes are blue,
yet bathing, the bright sun
deepens them. The eyes are her own,
not violet for nothing. I will leave out
the lips, for these the light has forgotten.

REQUIEM

FOR

CHRISTINE

LATROBE

And we will all be together in torment and so we will not need to remember love and fornication, and maybe in torment you cannot remember why you are there. And if we cannot remember all this, it can't be much torment.

Tragic wisteria nodding compassionate
lighter-than-lilac heads, bindweed, convolvulus,
you too to be reckoned with. Perverse,
flourishing at dockside to beat Hell. I am unsure
you are not spirits transplanted from some
careless purgatory short on space. I suspect
your flowers whirled first out of the sea mist,
then the umbilical vine
last shooting its hairy tendrils into the loam.

She loved you like sisters. You would make secrets
of each individual sorrow and hide them all
so, in that camouflage of constant mourning,
as darkly for a thousand colorless corpses as for none
run aground on the Patapsco banks.
Coast guardsmen root them up out of the sand,
jerk back the drenched heads by the hair and leave them
unidentified, faces worn smooth
as quartz rubbed pearly at a creek's bottom.

One of those wrecks I hereby claim
while scavengers claw the sand-bars for a shell.
Our single spirit is fit to be tied
with my shiftless half of its body still at large.

In that house skirted with green awnings, in the room
with awnings that looms above the harbor, shady-eyed
like a visored money-changer in a penny arcade,
they have gathered to find you dead there,
the prolix and fugitive tenses of your soul

finally calm and collected. Puffed eyes
of the matrons run, the lids rubbed raw
with mascara grit, men's cambric
handkerchiefs soggy with sweat. Over the door
a stone cross-eyed screech owl winks from the spandrel.

There will be words. And none of them
will dare the truth, that they were not robbed
merely of the corpse, but that for sure
no respectable death would visit there
to flatter that coffin of flame-grained mahogany
prone on the pallet, vacant and gutless, or add
a faint bloom to the steaming rose's cheek.
They would have doctored the honest death out of her,
injected a bloodless smile into the lips
and stretched her out in effigy. Better lost,
sea-weed winding the swollen veins,
eye-sockets granulated with sand pulver, the clabber flesh
pickled in natural solutions.
They don't care what death is or what it means.

There is so much I fear
you would not dare. I fear your soul
evaporated from the earth half-heartedly
leaving a sea-nettle grey residue
adrift in this heaving backwash still sensate.
And I keep fumbling after your last wishes.
Did they drive at death head-on
or finally turn, tug shyly at his sleeve,
the pain of fear outscreaming all the pain
that sent you there? But death holds out
its crash course, for authentic inductees,
in the language of unearthly things. Tottering

with you on the wire I may share
the nightmare of your fall, as unsure
of my next breath. Yet I'm denied the last
flash that burns all shadows from the truth before
you land wide of the last-minute net.

Rust-bound dredges in the harbor-mouth,
barges girded with black links of tire bumpers,
slanted derricks tilting at the sun.
Watching along the pine-cord wharves
for that sign you promised you would send
when the good times had all gone out of us.
But there are so many yours might be
lost in the rush or is it that
the time still hasn't come? We have promised
and been sworn so many things.
I may not have believed you when it came.

I have gone out in the streets looking for it,
peeping through newsheets riddled at the seams,
an apprentice hawkshaw periscoping street corners
with half an eye. The shrill vendor parading
his mare-drawn cart stacked with yam-crates, strawberries,
bumped on his good leg swinging a cloth-yard of space
from the street to a nervous thigh stump;
a blind drunk murmured into an ash-can
trying to wake an echo up
from the pit of dead metal—any ghost of a voice
not his own—that might
make loneliness something other than just
talking to himself. I heard this dream
turned on with a mystical hymn-like resonance
and lost bitching in the cavernous drum.

And turned back to the waterfront with no more sense
than those professional mourners of what was lost
and a damned sight less
idea what deserves the curse of being forgotten.

When time dies I know every second of it
must rattle off into Hell
for reminding men what is never too soon
wrecked and done with. I take it all back,
all my lies against your will,
though there were times when the gods I swear
seemed to whisper through my fingertips, touching you.

The Falls let down its black alluvion
from Harford Run to South Street long ago
hardened the river's arteries, gathering reefs
like broad-cloth ripples when drawn, or each thought
wrinkles its author's forehead, isolate and frail.
High tide swamped these until the shoals
bedded down and fly-by-night islands became fast land.
The brackish stream ran sapphire clear among them
and shark teeth of the schooners' topsails
of Guttro and Blanc, ran, that cut best behind the wind.
Those French merchants your ancestors kept their faith,
driven to each makeshift tabernacle
from the last, by pioneers in God's new holy land.

If your remains demand a charnel house I'll rent
the memory of St. Peter's chapel, snatch it
floating transparent up Charles Street, naked
tracing arrowtip steeples in the air,
and with no walls that stand to contain you.
I would prefer to have us both, who split

the live and dead worlds between us,
knee the rotted altar of some haunted church
in mind, that cannot scare the gods away.

My thought sends word it is hidden in my heart
but does the heart sound empty? What is that light
that shines on/off in the distance so persistently
flickering? Where is the pure mothering black-light of
     grief
that lights bones up from the inside, ultra-violet,
and rots the heart's teeth?

From the spare room of this world
I kept my vigil armed with one frail thought.
Where there is real tragedy is no terror
and no pity. The wild prayers
I have withheld for you
whose longing silence must outdistance death.

CATHEDRAL
STREET

Madonna (With Child Missing)

Shouts from the street, spotlights crossfire
at a third story window. The woman
stares through smoked glass at a crowd
and firemen in glazed slickers—
flames climbing the stairs behind her two at a time.
She lifts up the window sash with one hand,
kisses the infant and rolls it out trusting the air,
the soft knock of skull on stone in her heart.

The Jewelsmith's Last Apprentice

No seed of scrap platinum left to spring
light from the crucible's matrix;
I've scraped the chalk-flat porcelain clean,
laid his tools out: copper pickle tongs,
clock tweezers, pitch tongs and the dapping die
nearly leap from the selvedge cloth and shine.
One hour since dawn and the bench is set,
ready for the master when he comes.

Though there's no depending on a man that old
and I might well be sleeping.
Not so much his memory as his life I doubt
today, with this maddening necklace to cast
for the councilman's new lady, whose white throat
blinded the brightest pearls I tested there.
The blue tear of flame that tips the gas torch
goes glassy in the stronger light:

he's late. All I can do is save his steps,
leave no quarrel for his hands
that mine might settle, set out the vials
of ground cobb, that bleeds the sweat out of the gold,
steel shot for roughing the stones slick, enamels
that whirl a pin-wheel palette in the brain,
sheepskin and canton flannel buffs
that tickle the delicate rubies into flame.

What time's lost makes work the longer, I must
set all the matter closer to his mind,
let the stones loose, save him the detail

of folding and unfolding diamond paper, fiddling
locks, the numbers click off in my head,
there—four turns and tumblers trip, the crossbar falls!
Two black boxes slide from a deeper vault,
jewels wrapped square in glazed tissues crackling

in my fingers under the arclight, sapphires
from Kashmir, chipped off a brick of fallen heaven
in late evening when planets glow dim,
amethysts strained from violet-stained sand
in Rio Grande do Sul, pigeon-blood rubies.
And like stars sprung from glass uncracked by hail,
the shivering wreckage of some mad god's ideal,
diamonds whose cold sparkling stings your eye.

What will suit this lady? I heard
her ask for a corsage of violets and musk rose
in cold stones; if she knew
how tortuously the bush these grow from breeds!
They ask for the sudden flush of the true rose
without penalty of death wish or thorn.
Let's have an emerald for each mistress that she rivals,
a string of duck bone jade and blister pearls.

There will be little left for him to do
if my piece displeases him. He shouldn't be
so old as to forget that he is old and leave
a young man waiting hot to take his place.
So I am master of this work, unchallenged,
but where is my apprentice? Off
to steal the lady that it's fashioned for?
There's no relying on tomorrow's youth.

If she could know who had transformed
in one lightning collision all this gold and silver
to a battle of the sun and moon,
and the sky blown wide with stars!
The necklace must burn low on her breasts,
with such sweat my hands have bent the yielding gold,
how could she not love me feeling
the press of my passion and genius in its shape?

Two Middle-aged Women Confront
the Apparition of Old Hagar

Sally say your beads here comes old Hagar
hobbling witchlike, shaking like a linden,
her shoulders in time with her knees.
She's toting that book and black bag, mumbling
her tunes of cradles and the words of tombs.

White cap and gown
      in and out of season,
black hood and veil
      dead or alive.

Her staff is a wizard's wand,
her bag a budget of charms
and roots and herbs for the easing
of back pain and short wind.

  Hag of evil eye to the crones,
    fairy godmother to all children—

Sally shall we speak or run and hide?

Miss Ellie's 78th Spring Party

Miss Ellie rattles the champagne glasses
like crystal ghosts that tinkle when they touch,
to hail the Main Line in for Spring
at the last minute. There isn't much
time to call the company to come;
this year she has forgotten everything.

Picasso's dancers shiver in a frame
next to the window. Spring as well
seems to have forgotten itself.
Several curios upon the shelf,
a lion and a girl in porcelain,
tumbled when an icy draft rained in.

She wondered for a moment who would come
this year; though she'd forgotten, who'd recalled?
She forgot again what day it had become.
All the tenses moved two ways at once,
past and present standing back to back
moved through each other with no deference
to Spring or Miss Ellie. She is young and old
alike and won't remember which is when.
The company will be arriving soon
                                    and then
everyone has gone off in the cold.

Fire froze in the chimney. The first cork
exploded from the bottles, aimed to blast
a marble frieze of Pan upon the stair
and everyone who ever was was there
to breathe the spirits moving from the glass.

First Precinct Fourth Ward

Every bar on The Block shut down.
Villa Nova, the Crystal, the Ritz and Midway,
dead neon, night flowers gone day blind,
eyes like a gutted steeple,
streetwalker with her make-up peeled clean.

        The paradise is no more artificial
            than the money paid out for it.

Get your morning hot-dog at Pollock Johnnie's
      but don't ask for a drink.
This is the blade of justice untempered.
                  No truth in wine?
No more truth anywhere in town:
          when a man can't get booze on The Block
at a reasonable hour, or an unreasonable hour,
when a sailor can't go for broke on East Baltimore Street
      after a dry month at sea,
when a man can't get shot on East Baltimore Street
      for minding someone else's business,
a sailor can't get stoned, layed, blown and rolled
      for his pay
then we must look elsewhere for The Republic.

Blaze Star, where has she gone,
      and Lola, that up-side-down girl
and a hundred others that dance the drinks off the bar-tops,
      and the topless shoe-shine girls,

and the shades of countless women trapped in the photo
      peep shows?
They have all gone to the polls.

Jimmie the Greek is laying one hundred to one
      the President can't lose,
and the action is slower than a drugged clock,
      and may be slower.
But some people will bet on anything.

LETTER

CONCERNING

THE

YELLOW

FEVER

The disease called the bilious remittent or Yellow Fever is a disease of climate, unconnected with a foreign origin. This may appear to you a novel opinion, but my reasons for it are strong and shall be furnished for your consideration if it should please God to spare my life until I have more leisure . . .

To Edward Johnson, Esquire,
Mayor of the City of Baltimore

September 20th, 1818

Good health to you today sir and excuse
my want of promptness in this hectic time.
Your letter has overtaken me just now, the servant
eased it swift into my pocket
on the stairs to my first sleep these last two nights.
I am just come from the bedside of a girl
late visited with distemper, and have yet
to put her from my thoughts. The eyes bloodshot glared
at me, as though I were to blame
for the barb in her liver and gum swelled in her jaw.
And when I thumbed her eyelid back upon the ball,
the tongue lay so foul in the gutter of her mouth
I bid her clamp the lips over her teeth
to spare us the dread vapour.
She threw herself from side to side in bed,
her head like a coin just knocked and slowed
from its upright spin. I swear sir
I could hear her heart beat cross the room,
yet had to pinch her wrist for the softest pulse.
I drew thirty ounces of blood at a bleeding
to unfold the circulation and as mean
to the operation of her medicine:
six grains of tartar steeped in bone set tea,
spiritus mindereri cut with sweet spirit of nitre
and black snake root tea to open wide her pores.
I must return there in four hours time
between moon-set and day-break to see
what miracle I've worked.
Twixt now and then I'll set down all I can.

33

You know the great body of this city stands
on high and commanding ground, rolling
south where the land's peak stabs into Morgan's Cove,
the jagged outline of the wharves
like the apothecary's drachm mark *in extenso*.
So you see we are almost completely surrounded by water.
In summer such rank miasma clouds the point
that all but true natives of the Block are forewarned
to pinch ground garlic and shag tobacco up the nose
to choke back poison that would enter there.
Each June they scare some novel scapegoat:
ten years ago the pumping of bilge water and discharge
of ballast from the ship United States
that festered bare in the sun's eye near Pitt Street.
Now they accuse a parcel of putrid wheat
passed by when a ship's cargo was hauled ashore,
and left to soak in brine flooding the hold.
These are the same philosophers who chew
peach sprouts for ague, and probe their carious teeth
with splinters of sycamores struck low by lightning,
certain the charred pick must kill the nerve!
Next they'll blame the rotting carcass
of some dog rolled by schoolboys in the mud
or a poor hump-backed hag
who's let her wash hang out too long.
Yet give ear to these sir,
for they are not so wide of the mark
as certain of your august professionals.

I beseech your patience for what gall
may color a weary man's pen scrawl at midnight.
We would gladly set all blame for this horror
on our remotest enemy. Yet those

who have scouted its trail through the body
and plotted its terrible course on the map of land
know that the plague thrives in isolation,
is seasonal, and brewed at home.
Now certain high medical authorities
who sit down in their closets
and wrap up nonsense into an imposing shape,
will declare the wharves merely the lobby of contagion,
an innocent port where the alien disease puts in
to be distributed like so much freight.
These are sly tricksters wooing
our dull eyes to the shining goose in one hand
that will become a buzzard in the other,
whisking us past that black veil of exchange.

Two hundred tallied dead there in a week.
Those of us who schemed
to cheat the fever of its crop took note
of an uncommon green cast
to the dock waters in the plague's rage.
And an odor of cold damp cellars, putrid fish
or fowl's entrails rose from the water
like steam from a bubbling cistern.
We judged this a species of vile vegetable ferment
(you've seen how short a time it takes
wood to spice fresh water in a clean bucket?)
and ordered the harbour's derelicts towed and burned,
decaying arcs, hulks, masts and spars.
Yet this failed to slow the fever's pace
and all our wreckers caught the plague and died.

We did not know as yet the very earth
we walked upon was poisoned. The streets

of Fell's Point, the wharves and dock abutments all ride
on low new-made ground, on loan
from marsh-water and drowned wood at a high rate.
Sir to make ground the way they do
is more perilous than to raise battlements
on layers of dry dirt and gunpowder!
Way out in the harbour they drive a circle of piles,
then choke the pit with green saplings and pine cord wood,
pine tops, old barrels, chips and sawdust, shavings,
veneered with a thin green sodded stratum of earth.
The redskins might have made a better job of it
who would have left it to God,
who would have put it off indefinitely.
God knows we have less use for man-made land
than any tribe of men who ever lived.

As for the doctrine of contagion!
Those idle speculators who deal in it
for their share of the merchant's profit
will have a dead cart creaking under the weight
of this strange species of harvesting
to carry with them to the courts above. Although
perhaps they can gain no case so priceless
as that when the Yellow Fever was blown
from the docks to the senate chamber in Charlestown,
striking the winded delegates down in midspeech
until they lacked quorum. The survivors then
entertained the motion of abandoning
a country on which the judgements of heaven
must fall with so heavy a hand.

Yet such faith the people have in your provision,
they would have a man whipped through the streets

who would charge you with starting at a phantom
while a flesh and blood demon lodges in your house.
Why do they expect you to be versed
in those coy arcana of nature, heavenly laws
that strongarm matter, constant in causes
both friendly in man, and fatal?
You know no more of sickness than the wheelwright
who knows only when he is well,
no more than a carpenter knows of law
and the benign herding of men, who feels it
only when his next peg-nail is taxed out of reach.
But will men have you to hang the effluvia
between heaven and earth for a season
and give it no true origin—no progenitor—no abode
thereafter—neither author nor finisher?
Will you sit back and fold your arms, resigned
that he is a "demon that moves in darkness,"
contenting yourself to do nothing
because he is sometimes merciful?

I fear you haven't drawn
the circle of your advisors wide enough, or that
you have let treacherous quacks hang on your ear:
perhaps the leeches of a group of merchants
who have something more at stake
in this matter than their lives, or the lives
of anyone, and who beside
maintain estates for refuge in the county?
Well let them mark they look not far enough
in their own interests! Would they choose
to pick the pockets of rank corpses
and worry with dusting the wallets with gunpowder
to singe clean the money they infected first?

Lately a milliner sent
his apprentice to call on a shopkeeper in arrears.
Three times the boy knocked hard at the oak door,
that opened at length on a man with death in his face.
And when the child recited the sum of money owed,
this living ghost replied:
"call as you go by at Cripplegate Church
and bid them ring the bell," and with this said,
he shut the door, stomped up the stairs and died.

Sir I would train the coldest eye on all of this
as befits the case at large,
but for those cases we cannot serve without
recall to the roots of passion. These sprout alike
into the quick of each of us, in a few certain ways,
though our faces reveal only the flower and leaf.
A happy loophole in the contract
designed to make each man his best friend's mystery,
most fortunate for our craft!
For we are men first that we might become physicians,
and never turn the balance of this debt.

It is late at night or I would blot much out
and pen this whole epistle over again.
No shriveled crone schooled in backwoods witchery
or drunken sexton who's a friend to death
eyes my skill with such high contempt as life itself.
My hand always trembles when I attend her alone,
as now, with no struggling flesh there to distract me.
She smiles when I instruct her how to live.
Do not smile. There's not one man sick
but an entire city, and the plague threatens to leave
us without lives enough to bear the dead away.

I urge in short
you bid the merchants wall their docks in granite,
and burn some three dozen ships—
the poison greases their hulls like green sea-slime.
Let the pigs and cattle loose to root in the streets,
and discharge cannon at the break of day
where miasma is thickest, to shake it from the air.
Then there is that passage of Leviticus. Good health
to you again sir! I must return
before there is light to see my next patient dead.

William Martin
Fell's Point, Baltimore

THE

ASSASSINS

Thomas! I warn you
whistle twice from the high road—
I sleep with this pistol in my grip,
sleep less and less, dream none and wake up hard.
And the pain in my leg has run from a slow throb
to fits of shuddering in the damp.
A fine job he did, the good doctor,
the son of a bitch, if he didn't
set the bone to knit askew,
then turns me out to pitch in this gangrened sluice
and rest my head on a cold stone.

Pour me a half cup of brandy there
and take a short one to the boy.
        You see him through the laurel on his knees?
He hasn't moved for hours, and when I call
he starts and gapes as if I were a ghoul
or harpy riding the late night post from Hell.
        He will not drink? Well let him freeze.
His bent limbs will make fine woodland statuary
and put to shame
any limp-necked puppet dangling from a noose.
He served me well, Thomas, served me well.
Unroll the newsheets from your saddlebag
and hook the lantern on that hanging cedar branch.

Look here—they've sighted, handcuffed or shot down
a dozen counterfeits of me today,

the leg fractured in as many different places,
mustache peeled from the lip.
        What man is man enough to grant my courage
is welcome to the fame. They wrong me.
The yankees nod and dip their pens, headline
the wild cortege of my ancestry
(they're satisfied I'm lunatic by blood),
and cry "coward," black-tongued in the iron presses.
        No courage crusades outside of their law.
I wonder what the Richmond paper says.
They never praised my acting in the North.

They are an audience of basilisks
that drags to the theatre as some grave black mass
and won't sit still for any scene that lives.
No romance or heart-sound tragedy;
give them a dance of death or miracle play,
some tableau to stretch the conscience on the rack.
I played the scene they craved, to a broken tune,
dry organ snatches of the Miserere
that wailed from a hundred churchdoors at His death:
raw meat for the kites of guilt-scarred memory.
And still they carp and hiss. We cannot please.

And what man was this to name their God on earth,
who wears black gloves to the opera in New York
and has black guests to dine at the White House?
They would have made that bearded spider their next God
who dresses always in mourning.
I fear I might have played into their hands
by martyring him. Yet better
a martyr dead in heaven before his time
than a saint strutting the earth above the law.

That boy will deafen the delicate ear of heaven,
he prays with such a vengeance. And you know
he begs for nothing of good use.
For how could a merciful God deny
such devotion, and for what other kind
would Harold cramp his arms and legs that long?
Yet there he kneels, as if his only wish
were that he might continue praying there.
        What do you pray for Harold?
For your saviour to return to earth,
or for a place in some less clamorous Hell
where the katydids and birds are bound and gagged?

Oh Katy shall be free tonight and sing in the sycamores!
How you can banish sleep, quiet and good temper,
oh Katy how many nights have you kept me awake
cursing your strange monotonous shrill song!
        Now what do you pray for Harold,
do you want a place in history or in heaven,
a world of stress and battle and rare glory
or that tedious paradise for saints
turned out to pasture, the white celestial jail
of pitiless harmony?
Look how his hands tremble
welded at his palms, useless,
useless. No prayer will make them one.

Jimson weed and belladonna grow at my side.
And I have watched the red-tailed hawk at dusk
wheeling his watch above the black-slash pines
and yellow flickers in the buckthorn.
And I half expect some marvelous thought to pass
where never a thought has been before,

to shiver my soul like a wine glass, flawed and frail,
screamed at by a high strung violin.

    Oh Thomas you have lived
and taken life where it was not freely given:
what worth is the judgement of God or men,
what plush heaven or hell's broil, bribe or threat,
once a man has bought and paid for his own soul?

We dare not stir until the search moves North.
You must inquire where a man might send
word of an assassin's whereabouts
after the troops decamp from Nanjemoy.
If you should corner the major where he drinks
or meet him through the local whores,
don't look eager or you will be known outright.
He'll have learned of your former rebel sympathies
and distrust a sudden change of heart.
Act more as if you couldn't give a damn
to cling to some bygone dream
when there's a solid profit to be made.
No man will guess you would do otherwise.

    They say who breaks the silence feels
the brush of an angel's wing.
    I know there are no angels in this grove.
Your paper says the mark of Cain is on my brow
though not one of us has an eye for it.
And I'm damned for the deed that honored Brutus.
They've put a handsome price on my head, more money
than three virtuous men make in a lifetime.
    I swear I would rather see an honest cutthroat
grow fat on my useless flesh
than a trigger-happy deacon drunk on the voice of God.
    How can you afford not to betray me?

MOUNTAIN

AND

TIDEWATER

SONGS

The Exile's Letter

I first left the cities behind, then
the crowded wheat-fields, and last the women
because I couldn't bear their loneliness.
Far away they spin, behind me,
and the stuttering bells and hysterical sirens
speed out of earshot
wailing like deserted children.

Heaven still lies far beyond my means,
there are no vacancies in hell—
no goddamned place to go now,
not one blessed thing left to do.

And at this distance I'm no better
than a punch-drunk photographer, scrambling
in widening circles at a family reunion,
up and down on one knee,
telescoping the clustered generations
and defying their forced gravity.

Bodies crammed near static in the streets
await the plague winds of late spring:
cool air of death to stave off famine,

while I'm land-wrecked a few miles from water
feeling more happiness than they can know,
hoping that one straw of sunlight piercing a cloud
can prop the sky up for a few more hours.

Song of the Beekeeper

My bees gather the last winter store
from smart-weed, Spanish needles and goldenrod.
　　I will have my cup right side up
　　　　when the hives rain honey,
and men in town will pay for it.
　　They are afraid of the sting.
When I'm wiring the brood comb frames
　　and folks ask my business, tell them
I'm stringing the harp for my bees.

Song of the Sap Miller

Give us a southwest wind after the frost
      to set my trees all tingling in the grain.
Sun draw the sap up
            frost keep it down:
   no sap before light hits the frost,
   no sap when the cold is gone.
Kettles hang in the granite arch,
      a blue stream of smoke twisting skyward.
Smooth-skinned young maples start with high spirit,
fair on a run and flooding the keelers,
but they won't hold out.
      Now my thick-barked scarlet ladies
        do not shy at my auger.
I'll sink the elder spiles no deeper
   than your sweet white wood
and tickle the juice from your limbs.

Song of the Young Woman Gathering Ginseng*

I've been hunting ginseng since dawn
    from Sang Run to Backbone Mountain
untangling brush under red oak trees.
This virgin bed blooms with the five-fingered leaves,
and the berries! A berry for every flower.
My skirt is full of the spiral trunks, some
heart-shaped roots for the heart, spindles
that grind well for herb tea. But you
    little man, with your broad shoulders
and long tap root legs, you will bring
a pretty penny in the Chinese market.
Some lord will bid high to feel you under his belt.

---

* An herb found in the Allegheny Mountains, long prized by orientals for its curative and aphrodisiac properties.

Girl with a Lantern

The town is as empty of whores as a boy's choir.
They are all dead women.
Men stagger drunk out of bars,
dreaming lone jailbait on a back woods path,
cock-bait, whore's lure.

A barn lantern swings in her hand,
                a bell of light, out-shining
a moon so full it might spare
one blade for another moon to come.

*If she goes on a mission of life or death
let her pass*, the bushes rustling among themselves
whisper, and the woods push back from her path,
the town glowing high beyond. *Beasts
as terrified of beauty as men
would strike her as a blood-born enemy.*

Night Song from Backbone Mountain

Because you threw rocks at me on Backbone Mountain,
called me skinhead and my dog a bowlegged weasel,
don't come looking for me here to make up.
Go dig your own groundnuts if you can find them
        and onion weeds, and I hope
you choke on the buckbeans.

I'm nobody's fool, Jim Lewis.
I saw you lay her on the ground,
        your hands tangled up in her hair.
I saw you and I tried to run away
                up to Devil's Rock, up there
I watched her lead you back to town.

That is her way. I'm nobody's fool.
I know every bird here every leaf by names
        I gave them out of love, not
some name I stole from a book.
Every night I see the sun down
(you told me not to stare into the sun

        but still I go right on),
and I know my way by the stars.
No deer runs from me or wild turkey.
I live, I have been happy.
I'm nobody's fool but suppose I was
        and you were dead right all along?

A slant-toothed fool has his glory
        when banjos pick up in the bar,

and he dances for what dimes men toss on the floor.
They're his when he's done and gone home.

So long Jim Lewis.

I have been happy, so long.

Patty Cannon

Moon spun full in cold April,
frost on the blue-black skins
shivering chains in a thicket
of blackjack oak and white pine.

Cyrus Bell sailed up from Norfolk,
his satchel bulging with gold
to buy Patty Cannon's bootleg slaves
and smuggle them south in the hold.

Cyrus Bell rapped at Patty's door,
she led him down the hall.
"Could you trouble to put me up?" he winked.
"No trouble for me at all."

She set him a place at the window
to look on the dark broad yard;
she drew him an amber dram of rye
and set it down hard on the board.

"Those are stars that dance in the treetops,
it's too early for fireflies;
and those lights that glint in the underbrush
are whites of the niggers' eyes."

Cyrus Bell peered into the darkness
while Patty went for bread
she went for a matchlock pistol too
and buried a ball in his head.

She sacked his pockets and satchel
and carved him limb from limb;

she took him apart like a puppet
to fold in a chest of pine.

The chest was carved and painted
blue and glittering gold;
she dug him a grave in the April ground
and lowered him down in the cold.

She lowered him down in the April ground
and kept her slaves and the gold,
she dropped the chest and stamped the earth
but the grave didn't hold.

A ploughman was tearing the damp sweet ground,
cutting a trench for his seed
when the spring-toothed harrow kicked and snagged
on Cyrus Bell's death bed.

Patty is gone to the Georgetown jail
and a crowd trails howling behind.
She lies chained in the cold cell, curses
drift through the bars on the wind.

A good horse will see death in the distance,
a crow talks if you split his tongue,
streaks of light the clouds let through are pipes
drawing water to the sun.

Patty Cannon kept locked in an amulet,
a vial of black widow tea;
"if God hasn't struck me dead," she swore,
"no man will ever hang me."

Wild geese fled screaming the fallen sun
afire behind the mist.
The sun was done for, the western sky
held a glowing coal in its fist.

Song of the Hermit

Traveler beware, your cool grottos
hollowed in the world's side are my anterooms.

Sing clear of my range
or hear your song die fast on the air
like breath that clouds in the cold and vanishes.

There is no walking shadow in these hills
but mine; my dreams are singular.